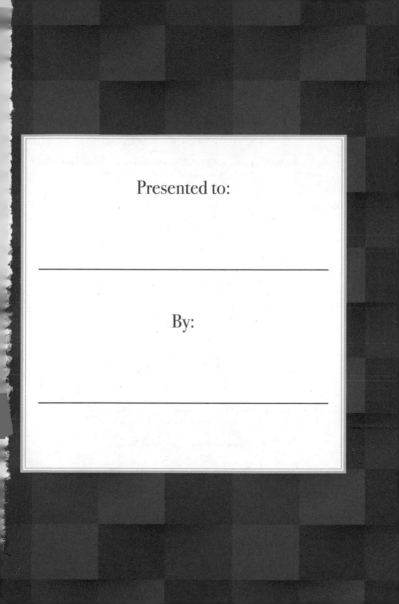

Presented to:

_____

By:

_____

Copyright © 2020 by John C. Maxwell

First edition: April 2020

Cover design by Jody Waldrup.
Cover copyright © 2020 by Hachette Book Group, Inc.

The Hachette Speakers Bureau provides a wide range of authors for speaking events. To find out more, go to www.HachetteSpeakersBureau.com or call (866) 376-6591.

The publisher is not responsible for websites (or their content) that are not owned by the publisher.

The author is represented by Yates & Yates, LLP, Literary Agency, Orange, California.

Faith Words
Hachette Book Group
1290 Avenue of the Americas, New York, NY 10104

faithwords.com

Faith Words is a division of Hachette Book Group, Inc. The Faith Words name and logo are trademarks of Hachette Book Group, Inc.

Print book interior design by Bart Dawson.

ISBN: 9781546017905 (Hardcover)

Printed in Canada

FRI

10 9 8 7 6 5 4 3 2 1

JOHN C. MAXWELL

WISDOM
ON LEADERSHIP

102 QUOTES TO UNLOCK YOUR

POTENTIAL TO LEAD

FaithWords

NASHVILLE · NEW YORK

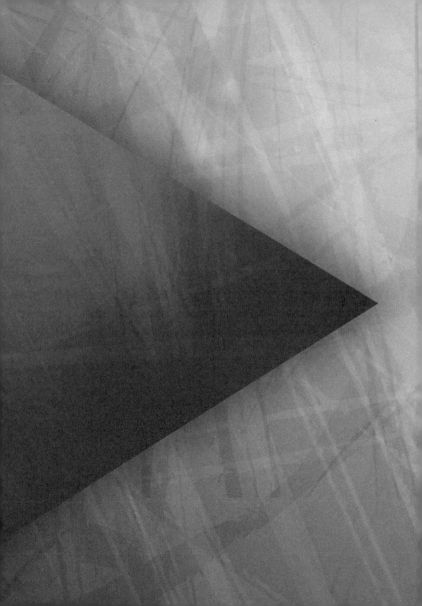

All you need to begin

is a **DESIRE**

to **LEAD**

and a **WILLINGNESS**

to **LEARN**.

There is no
clear path
to leadership.
There is no simple
checklist

for becoming a
leader.

Each person's
journey
is different.

Good relationships create
energy and give people's
interaction a positive tone.
When you invest time and effort to
get to know people and build
good relationships,

it pays off with greater energy
once the relationships
are built. And in that kind of
positive, energetic environment,
people are willing to give their
best because they know the
leader wants the best for them.

SUCCESS
means having those
closest to you **LOVE**
and **RESPECT**
you the most.

Movements
don't begin with the
masses—they always
start with one,

and then they
attract others
to themselves
and their **causes.**

With the right

ATTITUDE and

a **WILLINGNESS**

to pay the price,

almost **ANYONE**
can pursue great
opportunities and
ACHIEVE them.

RISK is always present in leadership . . . there is no **PROGRESS** without risk.

PEOPLE who want to make a DIFFERENCE

EXPAND
their worlds from
ME to *WE.*

Whether you are the official **LEADER** or you are just **PASSIONATE** about a cause,

you can work
with others to
ACHIEVE
a worthy **GOAL**.

Good **LEADERS** are always good **LEARNERS**.

I've found that the
worst thing
I can do when it comes to
any kind of potential
pressure situation
is to put off dealing with it.

If you **address problems** with people as **quickly** as possible and don't let issues build up, you greatly **reduce** their **stress** and yours.

The better the leaders are
in an organization,
the better everyone in the
organization becomes.

When productivity is high,
chemistry is good,
morale is high, and
momentum is strong,
then the payoffs increase.

Leadership is

DEVELOPED,
not DISCOVERED.

TRUST is required for people to feel **SAFE** enough to create, share, question, attempt, and risk.

Without trust,
leadership is **WEAK**
and teamwork
is **IMPOSSIBLE**.

Nothing
motivates
people in a
positive way

more than

seeing a

positive

leadership model.

You have to know
what you're
LOOKING for
if you want to
FIND IT.

If you want something
OUT of your day,
you must put
something **IN** it.
Your **TALENT** is what
God put in **BEFORE**
you were born.

Your **SKILLS** are what you put in yesterday. **COMMITMENT** is what you must put in today in order to make today your **MASTERPIECE** and make tomorrow a **SUCCESS**.

Good leaders see
their **ROLE** as
that of servant,
facilitator, value-adder,
success-bringer—

but they do this

QUIETLY,

without fanfare.

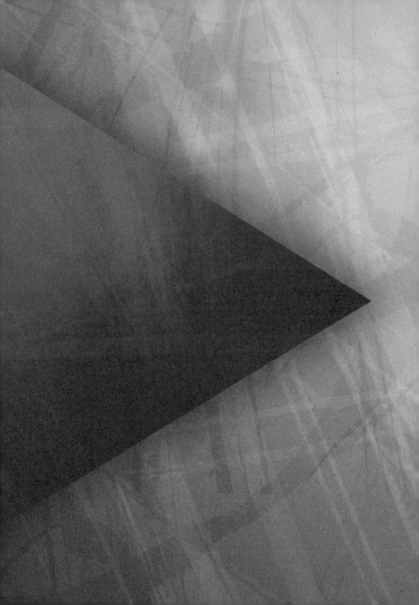

People don't care
HOW MUCH you
KNOW
until they know
HOW much **YOU**
CARE.

A **passive** life does not become a **meaningful** life.

You cannot make a difference if you stand on the sidelines.

Successful leaders
stay true to their
principles—to their
beliefs, gifts, and
personality.

They don't try to lead
in a style that does not
fit who they are.

The **UNEXAMINED** leader is not worth **FOLLOWING**.

Success
comes from
knowing your
purpose in life,

growing to your
maximum potential,
and sowing seeds
to benefit others.

The **ONE THING** you can do to have the **GREATEST IMPACT** on your leadership potential is to be **INTENTIONAL EVERY DAY** about becoming equipped to **LEAD**.

The true measure of success is **SUCCESSION**— what happens **AFTER** you're gone.

If we continue to hold
HOPE high, and
we help **OTHERS**
to do the **SAME,**

there is always
a **CHANCE** to
move **FORWARD**
and **SUCCEED**.

No teams win

CHAMPIONSHIPS

without

making
SACRIFICES
and giving
their **BEST**.

LEADERSHIP
is more
CAUGHT
than
TAUGHT.

Your ultimate **goal** as a leader should be to **work hard** enough and **strategically** enough

that you have
more than enough
to **give** and
share with others.

Leaders don't make excuses.

They take responsibility,
embrace opportunity,
and follow through.

VISION

is critical to

GOOD

leadership.

If you want to tap into
the **TRUE POWER**
of your leadership,
then you need to become
INTENTIONAL

about getting
BEYOND YOURSELF
and putting
other people **FIRST**.

People who wait for

the *one* great

opportunity

often keep

waiting.

The way to find
the **best**
opportunities
is to **pursue**
the **one** at hand.

Every time you **DEVELOP** a leader, you **MAKE** a **DIFFERENCE** in the world.

The better you
KNOW yourself and
the more **TRUE**
you are to yourself,

the greater your
POTENTIAL
for sustainable
SUCCESS.

ACHIEVEMENT comes
to people who are able to do
GREAT THINGS
for themselves.

SUCCESS comes when they
LEAD followers to do
great things with them.

But a **LEGACY** is created
only when leaders
put their people into
a **POSITION** to do
great things without them.

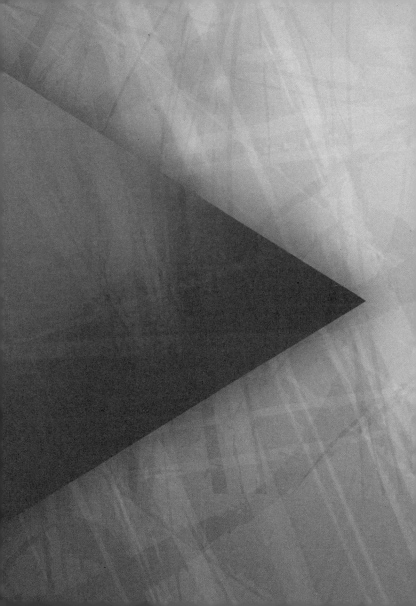

DOLLARS should **NEVER** be the primary **MEASURE** of **SUCCESS**.

If you want to be
successful
and reach your

leadership
potential,

you need to
embrace
asking questions
as a lifestyle.

Good leaders
understand that it is
their responsibility

to move toward

their people.

Leaders are initiators.

As a leader, you have to **SET** the **standard** and then **FOLLOW** **through** on it.

Successful people
do daily what
unsuccessful people
do occasionally.

They
practice
daily disciplines.

If you push yourself
to **DREAM** more
expansively,
to **IMAGINE**
your organization
one size bigger,

to make your **GOALS** at least a step **BEYOND** what makes you comfortable, you will be forced to **GROW**.

The best leaders **KNOW** what it's like to **FOLLOW** and have **LEARNED** how to do it **WELL**.

Success **DEMANDS** more than what most people are **WILLING** to offer, but not **MORE**

than they are

CAPABLE of giving.

If you **BEGIN** a task with **CERTAINTIES**, you will probably end in **DOUBTS**.

But if you are
WILLING to begin
with **DOUBTS**,
you will likely
end in **CERTAINTIES**.

LEADERSHIP is

DEFINED

by what a person does

WITH and **FOR**

OTHERS.

You can
like people
without
leading them,

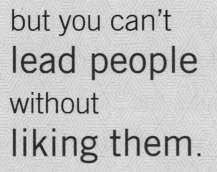

but you can't
lead people
without
liking them.

If you focus your
attention on a need that
speaks to your heart,
make the most
of your abilities,

tap into your passion,
and develop influence,
you can become
a leader.

Leadership isn't a right.
It's a **PRIVILEGE**.
It must be **continually**
EARNED.

When you **INVEST**
in another **PERSON**
just for the sake
of seeing that person
BLOSSOM,

with no thought to any
BENEFIT you might
receive, you will be
the kind of **GENEROUS**
person others want
to **FOLLOW**.

Good leaders think outside the box and help the team

break

through

barriers

and cover

new ground.

The mark of
someone with
POTENTIAL
to grow is
OPENNESS
to the process.

If you have
the **HEART** to make
a **DIFFERENCE**,
there is **ALWAYS**
an **ANSWER;**

if you have
a **HEART** of
INDIFFERENCE,
there is **NEVER**
an **ANSWER**.

GIVING people **RESPECT**
first is one of the
most effective ways of
interacting with others.
However, that doesn't
mean you can **DEMAND**
respect in return.
You must **EARN IT**.

If you respect **YOURSELF**, respect **OTHERS**, and exhibit competence, others will almost always give you **RESPECT**. If everyone treated others with respect, the world would be a **BETTER** place.

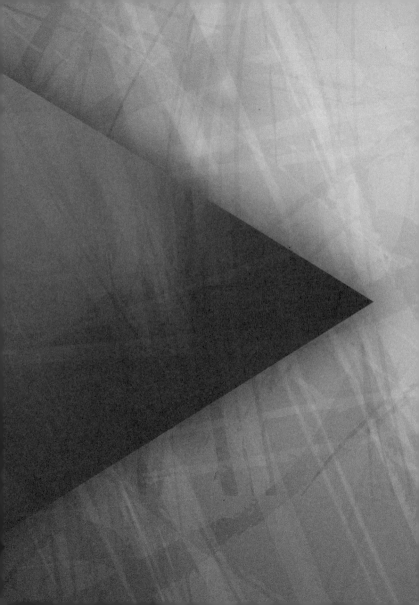

Leadership is a
PROCESS,
not a
POSITION.

Believing
in the cause
creates your
conviction.

Believing
in the vision
fuels your
inspiration.

Believing
in your people
builds your
motivation.

Leaders who rely on
their title or position
to influence others just
do not seem to work well
with people . . . they do not
lead well because

they fail to acknowledge and take into account that leadership—of any kind, in any location, for any purpose—is about working *with* people.

Successful leaders

work **HARD** to

KNOW themselves.

Good leaders
are able to look at
hard truths,
see people's flaws,

face reality,
and do it in
a spirit of grace
and truth.

Your **CHOICES** are
the only thing you truly
CONTROL.
You cannot control
your **CIRCUMSTANCES**,
nor can you control others.

By **FOCUSING** on your
choices, and making them
with **INTEGRITY**,
you control your
COMMITMENT.
And that is what often
separates **SUCCESS**
from failure.

Work isn't
WORK
unless you'd
rather be doing
SOMETHING
else.

CARE without candor creates dysfunctional relationships. **CANDOR** without care creates distant relationships.

But care
BALANCED
with candor
creates developing
RELATIONSHIPS.

Lead people **WELL** and **HELP** members of your team become **EFFECTIVE** leaders, and a **SUCCESSFUL** career **PATH** is almost **GUARANTEED**.

ACTIVISTS
don't merely **ACCEPT**
their lives as they are;
THEY LEAD
their lives.

Good leaders **stop bossing** people around and **start encouraging** them…

much of
successful
leadership is about
encouragement.

Leaders become great
not because of
their power,

but because of
their ability to
empower others.

People always
BELIEVE what
we **DO** more than
what we **SAY**.

If you want to become
a stronger leader—
to **LEARN**,
to **GROW**,
to **ACHIEVE**

your **DREAMS**
of significance,
and to make
a **DIFFERENCE–**
have **FAITH**.

Developing
as a leader requires
a combination of

intentional
growth
and leadership
experience.

Nobody gets
AHEAD
in life without
the **HELP**
and **SUPPORT**
of other people.

Good leaders
constantly
COMMUNICATE
the **VISION** of
the organization . . .

**CLEARLY,
CREATIVELY,** and
CONTINUALLY.

A leader's job is
not to know
EVERYTHING

but to **ATTRACT**

people that

KNOW THINGS

that he or she does not.

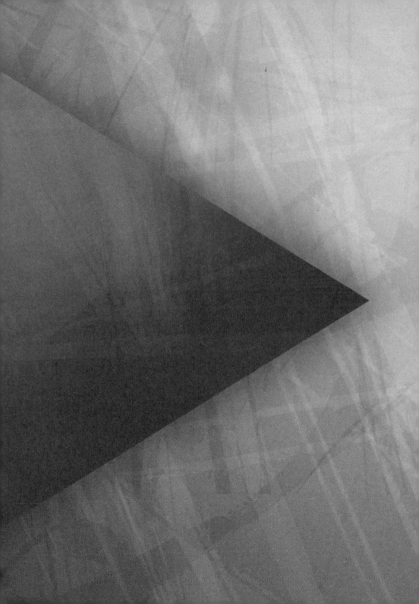

QUESTIONS are the **FIRST LINK** in the chain of **DISCOVERY** and **INNOVATION**.

Leaders
are always
taking people
somewhere ...

If there is
no journey,
there is
no leadership.

While personal maturity
may mean being able to
see *beyond* yourself,

leadership maturity
means considering others
before yourself.

Self-leadership . . . is
where **PERSONAL**
credibility is
ESTABLISHED.

Leadership
deals with people and
their dynamics,
which are continually
changing.

The **challenge**
of leadership is to
create **change** and
facilitate **growth**.

Leadership doesn't have to be **LONELY**. People who feel lonely have created a **SITUATION** that makes them feel that way.

Good leadership is
about walking
BESIDE people
and **HELPING** them
to climb up the hill
WITH YOU.

Your **VALUES**
are the
SOUL of your
leadership,
and they
DRIVE your
BEHAVIOR.

DREAMS are free.
However, the
JOURNEY to
fulfill them isn't.

You have to
WORK for
your **DREAM**.

Take a **GOOD LOOK** at yourself from time to time to **SEE** whether

YOU are
actually making
PROGRESS.

Good leadership **STARTS** with leaders **KNOWING** **WHO THEY ARE.**

If people are
willing to choose
improvement

and change
their attitude,
the sky is the limit.

Sometimes the smallest step in the right direction ends up being the biggest step of your life.

Tiptoe if you must, but take that first important step.

Self-leadership
comes **FIRST**.
It makes every other
kind of leadership
POSSIBLE.

Leadership **BEGINS**

with a **NEED**,

not when someone
wants to **FILL**
an empty leadership
POSITION.

Limited
influence,

limited
leadership.

Greater
influence,

greater
effectiveness.

One dedicated **PERSON** can make a meaningful **DIFFERENCE** in the **LIVES** of others.

If you want to be
SUCCESSFUL,

you need to
build on your
STRENGTHS,
not just shore up on
your **WEAKNESSES**.

If you make it your

GOAL to **EXCEED**

expectations,

you can **CONTINUE**
to learn, grow,
and **IMPROVE**.

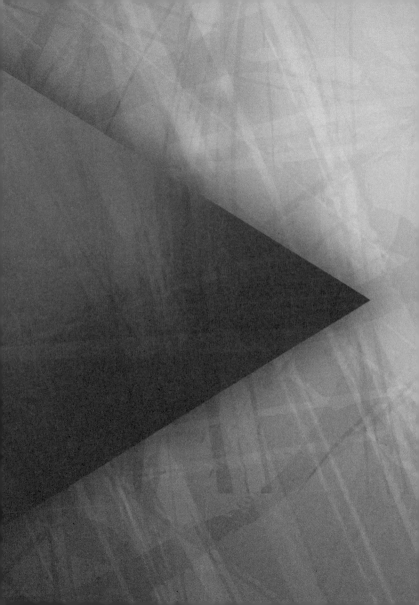

There is **NO JOY** that can **EQUAL** that of people working together for **COMMON GOOD**.

Good leadership isn't about **advancing yourself.**

It is about

advancing
your team.

Leadership is meant
to be active
and dynamic.

Its purpose is
to create
positive change.

Leadership **IMPACT**
is drawn not from
POSITION or **TITLE**
but from authentic
RELATIONSHIPS.

What got you
to where you are
today

will not get you
to where you
want to go
tomorrow.

SUCCESS comes when people work **TOGETHER**,

each person
PLAYING his or her
OWN PART.

It is impossible to **LIVE** a life that **MATTERS** and find **SIGNIFICANCE** without other **PEOPLE**.

PEOPLE don't expect their leaders to be **PERFECT**,

but they **DO**
expect them to be
HONEST.

Only by being **YOURSELF** and building on your **STRENGTHS** can you **BECOME**

a better **LEADER**.

The **BOOKENDS**
of success are
STARTING
and
FINISHING.

As the leader
of the **team,**
your **job** is to know
who is who, and
to **lead** the team

in a way that
maximizes the makers,
motivates the takers,
and **minimizes**
the breakers.